# A Letter to My Mother

# A Letter to My Mother

*Letters from Daughters Full of Love, Hope, Despair, Regret, and Forgiveness*

## CHARMAINE SHEELER

iUniverse, Inc.
Bloomington

**A Letter to My Mother**
**Letters from Daughters Full of Love, Hope, Despair, Regret, and Forgiveness**

*iUniverse books may be ordered through booksellers or by contacting:*

*iUniverse*
*1663 Liberty Drive*
*Bloomington, IN 47403*
*www.iuniverse.com*
*1-800-Authors (1-800-288-4677)*

*ISBN: 978-1-4759-7075-3 (sc)*
*ISBN: 978-1-4759-7074-6 (hc)*
*ISBN: 978-1-4759-7073-9 (ebk)*

*Library of Congress Control Number: 2013900475*

*Printed in the United States of America*

*iUniverse rev. date: 01/31/2013*

# Contents

## Chapters:

# Dedication

This book is dedicated to all of the people that we love and those who have taught us how to love.

# Acknowledgments

Our minds are as different as our faces, we are all traveling to one
destination—happiness—but few are going by the same road.
—Charles Caleb Coltan

To the lady writers—Chimére, Caren, Vickie, Sue, Lynette, D,
Betty, and the ones who chose to remain unidentified—thank you
from the "bottom of my heart"—for being so emotionally honest
and for being part of this project.

This is a little piece of our story.

You are such wonderful friends!

I would also like to thank the following staff at iUniverse,
Check-in Coordinator, Hope Davis, Editorial Consultant, Krista
Hill, Editor, Amanda and Publishing Services Associate, Jill Serinas
for taking such an interest in this project and guiding me along
with advice and their expertise.
To all of you that read this book, a little piece of our story. Thank
you for allowing us to enter your space and please join us!

# Preface

The idea to do this project came to me when I was speaking to my mother, who is in a nursing home and has dementia. At the very beginning of each conversation, I say, "Mom, do you know who I am?" One day, it dawned on and saddened me to know that the heart-to-heart conversation I always wanted to have with my mother was *never* going to happen. So I decided to write a letter to express some of the things I wished I would have had a chance to share. In the process, I decided to *invite* some of my dearest and most precious girlfriends to participate.

I am hoping that this book will help others who have something to say to their mothers and anyone they've ever loved and never had the opportunity.

# Introduction

This book is about the relationships between daughters and their mothers. It is not meant to judge mothers. Instead it is designed as a tool to help women understand their mothers and, realize that maybe they could have appreciated or loved them better or that they miss their mother because they never really had one. Our hope and desire is that it will help someone else and give someone the courage to write what may be hard to say. These stories are about life. They are in the form of letters that depict an acceptance of the way things are, possibly a clearer understanding of why some things were or a genuine and humbling understanding regarding the person the authors knew and loved as their mothers.

This is not the first time this topic has been broached, but the way it is being discussed is one of a kind. It is raw and it is honest. It is truth in its most basic form. These letters are not embellished; they are strictly from the heart and are memories that often flew below the radar or were forced to the surface. Those memories became so keen that it was almost too painful to recall them, let alone write them. Some of the loss and emotions are so strongly expressed that they are palpable.

All of these writers were assembled from women who have shared so many experiences in various stages of my life. I've known some of them since I was a child, whether I was a small child of six or thirteen. Some of the other women I've known since I've moved to this area of the country, and I've worked or socialized with them. However I met them, I love them all! We've shared many heart-to-heart chats, lots of laughter, and some tears.

Not all of the writers wanted to provide additional information about themselves because this experience has been highly personal and took us all on a long emotional journey to arrive at this point. I have rightfully respected their wishes and privacy, and I truly understand their desire for anonymity. As you will see while visiting with these writers and reading through some of these letters, some writers chose to do it because it was compelling or touching or because they needed to. I am flattered and very touched that they trusted me and knew I would treat their stories and hearts with love and respect.

I placed no limitation on the length of the letters. They are from the heart and one cannot hold in emotions that are erupting from one's soul to a page count. All of these letters were emotionally challenging to write because it required each writer to dig deep into that emotional well and retrieve thoughts and feelings that have long since become numb on the surface. Some of these feelings were bittersweet, longing, painful, forgiving, and sometimes angry. With the flood of emotions came questions, confusion, memories, gratitude, pride, regret, and lots of tears. I occasionally received cryptic messages from some of the writers expressing how hard this letter was to complete and the emotional rollercoaster they were experiencing.

As you continue to read along you will notice that some of these women have expressed how very much they miss their mothers. The longing is written with such fond thoughts that all you can do is smile for them because they are proudly carrying on the legacy of what their mothers bestowed on them at an early age. However, for other writers, it was a different story entirely. Not only did their mothers neglect them emotionally, but some of their mothers abandoned them. You will sense their loss.

While I was choosing my dearest friends to assist in writing this book, I daresay I learned a thing or two. Some of the lessons within the letters were eye opening and made me laugh, while others carried such an air of sadness. It is interesting to learn that something that you've buried down deep inside is often just that—"buried deep", it hasn't gone away at all. If you learn how to disguise your emotions at an early age, you get pretty good at it. It doesn't mean that it doesn't hurt as deeply as people who wear their emotions on their sleeves or even those who shout to the world that they are in pain. It usually means that you just don't show it as visibly, although internally you might feel as if a sharp razor blade is ricocheting throughout your entire body. You know that you dare not flinch—and mustn't show the pain—that you feel. You know that if you give into it, you will crumble and fall. Although your pulse might quicken—your feet might get cold—and your hands may be sweaty, no one knows but you. It's just another secret to add to all the rest. All you really know is you want a better life because you've seen it, you've visited it, and you even know what it looks like. So you focus on the positive, and like a good soldier—you march forward.

# Quotes

*Children* begin by *loving* their *parents*; as they grow older they
*judge them*; *sometimes*, they *forgive* them . . .
—Oscar Wilde

You will know that forgiveness has begun when you recall those
who hurt you and feel the power to wish them well.
—Lewis B. Smedes

Genuine forgiveness does not deny anger but faces it head-on.
—Alice Duer Miller

In the Bible it says they asked Jesus how many times you should
forgive, and he said 70 times 7. Well, I want you all to know that
I'm keeping a chart.
—Hillary Clinton

The weak can never forgive. Forgiveness is the attribute of the strong.
—Mahatma Gandhi

Yesterday is gone. Tomorrow has not yet come. We have only
today. Let us begin.
—Mother Teresa

# About the Author

Charmaine Sheeler is a native of Ohio and is one of ten children. She holds a bachelor's degree in psychology, graduated cum laude, and completed an accelerated paralegal course at Georgetown University. For the past twenty-one years she has resided in the Maryland/DC area. She lives with her husband, Robert Mitchell, a retired District of Columbia Metropolitan police officer, and she has three stepchildren. She has worked for the Federal Government in Washington DC, for twelve years as a paralegal and has a small business making handmade teddy bears and home décor. She does event planning on the side. Her hobbies are photography, writing, and traveling in her spare time.

# Definitions

| | |
|---|---|
| **Mother:** | a person who provides the care and affection normally associated with a female parent |
| **Foster-Mom:** | brings up a child that is not one's own by birth |
| **Adopted Mom:** | legally takes another's child and bring it up as one's own |
| **Ma, Mama, and Mommy:** | one's mother |
| **Daughter:** | a girl or woman in relation to her parents |
| **Love:** | an intense feeling of deep affection |
| **Adore:** | to love and respect deeply |
| **Abandon:** | to give up completely |
| **Neglect:** | to fail to care for properly |
| **Forgive:** | to stop feeling angry or resentful toward someone for an offense |

1

# Chimére

If it weren't for the ever-present text messages, I could pretend you don't exist. That's the only way in which we've communicated for the last three months. There is a slight tug at my conscience only because of those silly titles that will forever bond us. I am your daughter. You are my mother. I should be calling you at least three times a day to make sure you're doing well. You should be able to set your watch by the actual time of day I call just to say, "I love you." You should expect a quick call to check your clothing size so I can randomly pick up a special gift for you. In a perfect world, sending you a text message would be a last resort when my phone simply won't work on the subway or a plane.

But I don't need another reminder of the fact that this isn't a perfect world. For if it was, I would not feel this pang of guilt for not communicating with you as often as I think I should. I'm not too busy taking care of my own children; I'm not too tired from a long day's work; and yes, my phone is working better than it ever has. I'm almost glad you stopped calling me. I'm hoping the text messages will soon come to an end. I want to live in a world where people don't feel this insatiable need to ask if I have or haven't spoken to you. I wish I could stop myself from telling people, "Oh, she's fine," when I have no clue how you're doing—unless we count those few text messages you send informing me of your aching knee or of the latest book you bought written by Marvin Gaye's sister. And truthfully, I don't even know if I really care.

I'm sure I won't receive the 'Perfect Daughter of the Year Award.' There won't be any articles in our local papers profiling our great relationship. There are no photographs of us together that chronicle my changing hairstyles or your wrinkled smile. The last time we hugged was during the Christmas holiday. Someone recently invited me out for Mother's Day, and I actually contemplated going. Then it hit me: on this day, which is carved out for the mothers who make the world go round, I should at least consider spending time with you.

I keep trying to make my head, heart, soul, and spirit align when it comes to you. I have tried to will all four to work well together so we can have the perfect relationship, or at least the kind I can be proud of. But each time I think I can pick up the phone to call you or even drop by, I remember something repulsive you've said or how much you irritate me, and I quickly press the *end* button on my phone and shake thoughts of you away.

My brain screams that I should just make peace with you. You're the only mother I have. Unless some freaky switcheroo occurred at my birth, I am almost sure you're my biological mother. We have the same eye shape, and when we smile, our cheekbones try to reach the sky. My legs are long, just like yours, and our voices sound alike when we speak. Just because we are genetically related, I should want to love you. Yes, I know life can be hard, but loving you should be easy. It's only right that I acknowledge your role as my mother. You gave birth to me, for God's sake. You could have died having me and the least I could do is respond to those text messages or call you every now and again. Compared to the horror stories about mothers drowning their children in large bodies of water or placing toddlers in ovens to die, you are a stellar mother.

But I know better. And you do too. No physical damage exists to show the effects of our scarred relationship, but my emotional well-being is certainly bruised. The last time I checked, the only time the brain really shuts off is during sleep or death, so I think of you more than I care to only because my brain doesn't allow me to do much else when I consider what my family should be but clearly isn't.

I'm thinking of the people I love right now. Your name never appears first. I've been in some pretty intense love relationships with men that have set my heart on fire. When I love someone, you can tell. I move heaven and earth for them, or at least I sure try. My love consumes my every thought, action, and word. You knew how much I loved Kevin, my first love, because after finding secret love letters I had written to him in tenth grade, you spent hours on end telling me not to bring home a baby at sixteen. You knew I loved Aunt Tenie because even though she was seventy-five and I was thirteen, I enjoyed spending every summer with her without being forced. You even knew I loved Pastor Willie F. Wilson because when I was nine—even when you tried to block me from leaving the pew with your knee—it was his voice begging me to come to Christ that I ran to. And everyone knew I loved Earl; if it wasn't the fact that I talked about him all the time that gave away my secret, it became apparent in the twenty-five pounds I lost when he left.

My love is pure, raw, and real. It stretches past faults, mistakes, lies, and flaws. As a young woman not yet hardened by too many life experiences, my love is intoxicating and infectious. But you wouldn't know this, because for the last twenty-five years, you haven't experienced the purity of my love. I think of the few times I've heard myself tell you I love you, and I'm not sure I meant it. Perhaps I was saying it because I do really want to love you. What daughter doesn't genuinely want to love her mother? In those moments, I believed that saying the words would cause my heart to cover my pain with love. That must be how men feel when they say those words to a woman they know they can never love. Maybe if they say it enough, they will start to believe their own lies. Like theirs, my words feel hollow and untrue. I've had my heart broken by men who lie about their love for sport, so I have a hard time believing that when it comes to you, I can be that shallow. But as I think about, I have a hard time believing you've always been that shallow.

God's view of how I choose to handle our broken relationship scares me the most. As a Christian, I've read the Ten Commandments so many times that I can recite them forward and backward. One of them clearly tells me to honor my mother and father. While my father didn't log in enough parenting hours to get my esteemed honor, you've had a chance to earn it. And you've failed miserably. Somehow I don't believe God is taking my side on this one; no matter how many times I tell Him how much you've disappointed me, He still keeps urging me to reach out to you. But I am like the rebellious teenager; I hear Him loud and clear, yet I refuse to obey. While Jesus courageously forgave those who betrayed Him, shamefully, I cannot do the same. Only God knows I want to forgive you, and I know I've tried. The exhaustion of trying seems to have caught up with me. Ma, I just don't feel like trying anymore.

You have not been a good mother to me. There, I've said it. If I weren't so embarrassed about the backlash I would face, I'd purchase billboard space to let everyone know. If more people knew what a mediocre mom looked like, it would give women more incentive to think before they bring innocent children into the world. Maybe the reason I still don't have kids is because I've spent enough time babysitting you to know that my tolerance level is not high enough. Or maybe it's because I never want my children to feel abandoned or betrayed because I chose a man or money over them.

I feel responsible to you because of our assigned roles; I'm supposed to owe you something, anything, as repayment for your sacrifice to me. But since our roles are never really clear, I am usually confused. And they have never been clear. I've been your mother in thought and deed so much that I have a tough time reverting back to being your daughter. I don't remember what that feels like. Being your daughter is something I've never really been good at. I can sing, write, and speak pretty well, yet treating you like my mother proves the most challenging.

It's hard for me to forget handing over paychecks to you to help pay rent or phone bills before the age of eighteen. Money that I should have spent buying CDs, getting manicures, and buying the trendiest jeans, I gave to you, hoping you would buy food for Terrance and me. Well, Terrance was the one I was always worried about. He was a growing boy then, and I could survive off the greasy leftovers at Pizza Hut, where I worked after school. You always told me that when I started paying bills in your house, then I could do what I wanted. Funny enough, as the mother in our house in those days, I don't recall living as carefree a life as you promised. I remember feeling stressed, depressed, angry, and neglected. Do you remember seeing me this way? Or were you so consumed with your own life that you forgot about raising a daughter?

You lost her when you were about nineteen. I get it. You were her baby. Her Mutt. I've heard the stories time and time again. Six of you, and she loved you best. She gave you everything you wanted, rarely refusing you. And as you barely crossed the threshold of adulthood, she left you alone to fend for yourself. Cancer ravished her body, hair, and ability to speak. I've heard about how you sat by her bedside in the hospital for days at a time, sometimes forgetting to bathe. I also know that when she was permitted to come home to complete the process of dying, you bathed her and treated her like the baby you didn't yet have. Some people say that when she took her last breath, you screamed for her not to leave you alone and you wouldn't let your siblings take her body away from you until you grew tired of crying.

Even when I've asked questions about Frances Eloise Smith, I hear the twinge of sadness in your voice and see the memories in your eyes. I'll be thirty soon, so that means you lost her about thirty-five years ago. I can't imagine what that has been like for you. I can't imagine losing a mother. Moreover, I can't imagine loving you as much as you loved my grandmother. Somehow I can't help but think that losing her stunted your growth. She couldn't help grow you up, as I am sure she intended. Life met with death is funny like that. Yes, you've matured in some ways: you had two children, maintained several jobs, and are arguably functioning as a fifty-four-year-old woman. It can sometimes be so easy to do. But when I see you or hear your words, I often see and hear a hurting nineteen-year-old stuck in a painful-to-watch time warp.

I look at you and try to make myself be the bigger person. I tell myself a little joke to keep from remembering all the times I've had to be just so big just to keep from strangling you. The joke is if I don't start running again, I just may literally become the bigger between the two of us. But there is some illogical, insane gnawing in me that makes me want to try one more time, say one more nice thing, be this sweet daughter I never learned to be just so I can say I've done the impossible. Failure doesn't scare me because I've done it enough to know how it works by now. (Talk to my last boyfriend and he'll give you the scoop, Ma, I promise.)

In my mind, the tremor of maybe works in the grooves of my mind: maybe if I try hard enough, it will make you love me the way you should—the way your mom loved you. How is it that she seemed to love you like a big, warm sweater on a winter's somber morning, yet the love you've attempted to give me is nothing more than wrinkled rags with holes and stains? Is this your best effort? Could you not muster enough strength and courage to love me better than that? Is your definition of love seeing how far I will go to prove my love for you? Maybe that's it. And if so, I totally get it. I think. But are mothers really supposed to be these weak creatures who are incapable of finding some type of maternal strength to stand on? If I get any bigger in my trying, Shaquille and I will be neck and neck. I could use a few more inches of height, but I'm not sure it's ever been my wish to be that huge. But what is a woman to do? I'm just not the type of woman who can idly sit and do nothing, even if you deserve the nothing I won't do.

I know people who've been *abandoned* by their mothers by way of unadulterated *abandonment*, drugs, or alcohol. These examples of motherhood I've seen up close and personally. To the untrained eye, I look blessed; at least I knew where you were and are most of the time. I've never seen you take a toke of a cigarette or a blunt, and the only drink you'll have on rare occasions is a nice, cold Smirnoff Ice, and even that has to be flavored beyond oblivion.

So I'm lucky, right? What if I told you I think those others were even luckier? At least their mothers were usually out of mind and sight; they didn't taunt them with their presence. There is nothing more disturbing than sharing space with a mother whose eyes you can't read and whose love you can't find. A crack-head mother, in all of her selfish glory, is too busy looking for her next high or excuse to care about the well-being of her child. She can't fathom a world outside of her drug-induced comas, but she knows enough about her failures (and appearance) to maintain an unhealthy distance between her and her offspring.

But there were days when I was a girl when you were too tired, sad, or unavailable to just throw a pile of love on me. And you were there in my face, day after day, scowling at me to *perform this chore* or to 'be' this way. Looking in your eyes held nothing promising or rewarding that made me want to stay up under you after high school or return to live with you when times got extremely tough. You cooked dinners, you helped us with homework, and you even braided my hair, but there was a glare of fog around you that kept you from me. Maybe you should have just stayed away. Then I would really have an excuse to be the bad-assed daughter I could be. Yeah, if you had physically abandoned me, I could blame some of my greatest faults on you. Seeing you is a reminder of how much I can't erase the presence of this need I have to be loved by a mother I sometimes hate.

There is still a place in my heart open to receiving your love, just as I'm sure there are countless other children who feel the same. While I am growing in the strength that God and I have crafted, there is still a yearning weakness that troubles me: I long for your love. No excuses, apologies, or hindrances. There, I've let the cat out of the bag. I crave your attention, acceptance, and care even though I've learned to exist without it. Or maybe I have just been holding my breath and waiting for you to give me something you simply cannot because you and I are not the same. And this is where I've gotten stuck on plateaus where there is just my love and me: I forget to remember that everyone simply doesn't offer love in the same capacity as me. Even you, my mother.

Your daughter,

Chimére

# Conversation with Chimére . . .

## Why did you want to be part of the project and write the letter, and what did you get out of it?

My friend Charmaine helped rescue me from a dangerous place and person: myself. When our friendship began to take shape, I was exiting a relationship that turned sour, and I simply did not possess the strength, courage, or wisdom to move forward. Charmaine saw me through some of my life's roughest moment: the twenty-five-pound weight loss, erratic behavior associated with heartbreak, and my obsession with winning someone back who had no desire to be reclaimed. Having someone view me in this light while still believing I had the potential to survive and succeed was endearing.

One can't help but share other aspects of life while muddling through the rubble of lost love, and I am no different. Charmaine and I have talked too much not to discuss my childhood and my strange relationship with my mother. When she presented me with this idea, I trusted that she would take care of what I revealed, as she has with everything else I've entrusted to her within our friendship over the last six years. I also believe that a woman can suffer more loss at the hands of a troubled relationship with her mother than a romantic association. This was my attempt to shed light on this from my perspective. I needed to share what I haven't been able to articulate with one of my dearest friends—on paper.

I like my emotions like I like my television: in real-time. Writing this letter to my mom forced me to place no barriers between what I've felt for quite some time about my mother and me. With no one (even me) breathing down my neck, forcing me to be the perfect daughter or woman, this letter lifted the burden I have placed on myself for not feeling the normal euphoria and love toward my mother. In that moment, I was many things: the scared five-year-old girl, the self-assured adult, and the confused daughter. This letter gave me no hiding places and no room to be inauthentic or swayed by trying to say or do the right thing. It put me in the spotlight with my mother, even in her absence, at center stage. I even felt like I was wrestling with my mother or at least the words she would use in her defense of my rawest emotions. For me, there was no winner or loser; there was simply me owning my truth—in real-time.

I'm still hurting about my scarred relationship with my mom. I still want to crawl into her lap and have her rub my back to tell me that life will be okay. I'm learning that my existence is tied so much into the relationship that we could have shared. However, I need to remove myself from the fantasy of what could have been and simply accept what is and can be. Throughout this process, the word *forgiveness* keeps creeping into my mind. I need it all the time. And I've learned that the same person who needs to constantly be forgiven may need to learn how to extend the same gift to someone who may not even be able to express how much they need the same.

2

# Caren J. Gray

A Letter to my Mother:

Dear Mommy (a.k.a., Minnie L. Pringle-White),

*I love you and I miss you sooooo much.* It's hard to believe that you've been gone twenty-six years. You left me all too soon. Although I was a "grown woman" of twenty-seven, I actually really was not grown until that instant (July 26, 1986, approx. 5:00 a.m.). It was then that I realized that even though I had been on my own since I was twenty-two, I had yet to be on this earth a sufficient amount of time to acquire all the lessons, drink in all your wisdom, or draw in the soul of you. I would love to be even half the woman you were. I took so much for granted about what you said, what you did, and how you did things. If I could get back the years, days, hours, and minutes that I spent with you, I would have asked more questions, listened more intently, told you more how I appreciated you, and said I love you at least one more time.

I watched you throughout the years, and somehow you were able to do it all. Did you know you were somewhat of a "phenomenon?" As least I thought you were then, and now, twenty-six years later, I know you were. I'm still not sure how you did any of it. You were a single mother with five children, college educated, and always employed. You had two jobs most of your life and were never on welfare or what you called a handout. You always managed to make it front and center to everyone's games, recitals, plays, and most of the small and big moments that meant the world to us.

You were an amazing chef, baker, and caterer for all the parties and our famous Sunday—night snacks. And holidays . . . holidays were always *fantastic*! Even though we did not get big gifts or take an expensive trip every year, we learned what it meant to have family, love, and encouragement. That lesson was invaluable. Hands down, you were the most giving of your time, your heart, and a lot with your car. You played cab driver for us and the neighborhood kids, getting us to the high school games, practices, and of course not just church but Sunday school. You sat through night after night of reading bedtime stories, doing hair, washing, ironing, and many, many hours of homework. Reluctantly, I know, you let us keep those stray dogs, rabbits, and dozens of goldfish and turtles just because it made us happy, and through that we learned the lesson of caring for something or someone other than ourselves.

We were always your priority, your world, and I am sure it cost you many relationships or blinded you when you made the choice to be with the one who said, "I'm here for you and your kids." You did not always put these things into words, but I knew even at eleven years old that was what you were trying to do.

So, Mommy, this is what I learned from you and have learned since. Even though you have gone, you are still teaching me your lessons through your spirit. Have faith in a higher power, but always believe in yourself, trust your gut, honor your elders and your parents (live or in spirit), and give respect to your family. Strive to excel, push to get your education, and use that as power to move forward in life. Don't allow others to make you a victim or cause you to look over your shoulder because you were not doing what was needed or what was right. In the end, you only have yourself to answer to. Have a path and a plan for your life. Even if that path is just to be a good person. Make decisions you can live with. Primarily, get along with others in order to get on with your life, friendships, relationships, and even your job.

In closing, I pray that you are proud of the daughter, woman, sister, auntie, wife, step-mother, and nana (a.k.a. Grandma) I am or am trying to be.

Sadly, now that you are gone, the biggest lesson I have learned is to *listen* to that voice that I now know is you in *spirit*. You are always there talking to me, guiding me, and telling me . . . *trust me!*

As I look in the mirror, I see you looking back at me. The same is true when I look at my brother and sisters, my niece and nephews, and their kids. I see some part of your personality. They may use phrases that radiate that your spirit is there . . . *always!*

Love You,

Caren

# Conversation with Caren . . .

## Why did you want to be part of the project and write the letter, and what did you get out of it?

First and foremost, I was asked by my dearest friend in the world if I would be interested in a current project she was embarking upon, *Letters to My Mother*. Writing a letter to my mother sounded like a beautiful tribute. It was also something I had not done in a long time. My mother was an avid writer. As a teacher, she loved to write. When I was in college, my mother would write some of the most beautiful letters that it would just bring you to tears. This project just so happened to come along during the twenty-sixth year after my mother's passing. This letter is dedicated to her life.

It has been twenty-six years since my mother's passing. As hard as it was to write this letter, it also was a healing process for me. I have spent the last four years doing some self-discovery and reassessment of my life. I have been assessing what is truly important. One important thing on my professed bucket list was to reconnect with the spirit of my mother.

The principal thing I got out of writing this letter was that I am much stronger then I give myself credit for. I had to dig deep in order to stay in control. It took me some days to complete the project because writing this letter stirred up so many emotions. I am always afraid to open up about how I feel about my mother. It is hard to share what she meant to me—what her death meant and how it molded the rest of my life. I learned that my mom reveals herself to me in many ways in my world. I have now learned to pay attention. Writing this letter was in and of itself her redirection of my thoughts and my life and reconnecting with her spirit.

3

# Vickie

A Letter to My Mother:

I want to thank you for giving me my life and for caring for me and all my siblings in those early years, just beyond memory. I feel a great capacity to love, and I feel loved by all my siblings, so much so that I know you met our needs the best you could in a very difficult situation. Thank you for that.

"Happiness is like the enchanted palaces we read about in childhood-where fierce dragons defend the entrance and approach, and monsters of all shapes and kind require to be overcome—before the victory is ours and we arrive."[1]

Thinking about writing this letter to you—my mother—made me think of this quote about happiness. I am sure one's childhood should not cause this sort of musing. I remember well your gentleness and softness but also your fear and fragility. I think I felt afraid before most other feelings came into my awareness. Early echoes of angry words—not yours but those directed at you—and the loudness that universally frightens children brought with them a cold wind and steady anticipation of problems.

---

[1] Dantes in Alexandre Dumas, *The Count of Monte Cristo*. (France: 1844-46), chapter 5, page 47.

I remember your touch as kind, an attempt to give security where you felt none. I would feel your restlessness, you were young and beautiful, but your life was not. I have a memory that recurs from time to time. It was a car ride home from the Piggly Wiggly grocery store. The brakes were going out on the car. How much like life that car seemed to me—out of control and racing along. But I also remember believing there was a way? When you left us in the turbulent '60s, I held the hand of my little brother, and as he crossed his fingers to begin his waiting and watching vigil, I feared you would never return. The times when you did come back briefly, I think I remember feeling hope . . . maybe you could stay. But it was not to be.

This letter is a reaching out to say all is well. I am well, and I can hope for your ability to be happy. I pray you can and have forgiven yourself for leaving us. If you have not, know that God forgives freely, and so must we, even if it is ourselves we need to set free. When we met in 1986, I was happy to be able to see you and tell you that I did forgive you and wish only good for you. It was easy because I always saw you like us, young and vulnerable.

I've often thought the worst thing about growing up the way we did was the absence of good memories—those things I supposed you could run to as an anchor during hard times. In life's storms, memories are the things—the thoughts and feelings—you can go to for comfort and strength. I believe that is one of the reasons I never looked back much. I felt I had to always keep going ahead. I want to make sure you know I did forgive you. After Arthur died, it became clear to me that I needed to completely deal with the past and lay all the burdens at the cross, where I found forgiveness and life.

It was so good to see that you were OK—that you had people in your life who loved you and you could love in return. Even though, for whatever reason, we did not progress to a relationship as we might have—it was all right—it was enough. I only wish the best for you in this life. Yes, it was frightening when I was very young with no safe landing place. The Ohio Soldiers and Sailors Children's home did that for us. It was there that my heart did what my tongue could not—cry out with a great and bitter cry to the one more ready to hear than any other, "Oh God, take care of me." And he has.

I look back with sadness for all we lost and never will recapture, but it really is well with my soul—and may it be for yours also.

Your Daughter,

Vickie

4

# Lynette A. McMillen

May 2012

Hi, Mom,

I talk to you a lot, but I haven't written to you in a long time. There are a few things I want to say to you, and some things I have said but they warrant being repeated. In this case, I don't think you will mind me being repetitive!

You were always my mother, even when I didn't always make it easy for you. I volunteered you to be room mother, chaperone, and the driver for the carpool, and if we would have had soccer teams back then, I would have volunteered you to be a soccer mom!

You picked me up when I failed and applauded when I succeeded. I will never forget my sixth birthday. You and Dad gave me a new bike. It was perfect! So perfect I would not let anyone else ride it. When you realized this, you consoled my friends and asked me to look through the window in my bedroom. As I opened the curtains, I saw each of my friends having a turn riding my new bike. After I finished crying, I asked you why you let everybody ride my new bike. Your answer was, "We are all God's children, and God would never deny anyone a ride on a bike—especially one he is letting you use until you get older." I will say one thing—I learned to share!

Now I'm sharing some of the lessons of life you taught me to those who will read this letter.

You were always honest with me, even sometimes when I really did not want to hear it! When other children were teasing me, you would hold me and tell me everything would be okay. You would tell me that they were just jealous and teasing me was the only way they knew how to express that. Then you listed all of the attributes I had at the time and told me how proud you and Dad were of me.

When I teased the girl next door, you punished me for hurting her feelings. I asked you why I was being punished for teasing and they weren't punished when they teased me. You said I was being punished because I knew better. Then you made me recite the golden rule. Today, I try to be conscious of others' feelings.

As I grew older, you were not just my mother; you became my best friend also. You listened to me when I voiced my insecurities as well as when I voiced my self-pride. You were there when I fell in love and when my heart was broken. You were there when I broke someone's heart and helped me do it without tearing down his ego. When I had an argument with a friend, you never hesitated to tell me when I was wrong, and you *always* understood how I felt.

You always allowed me to follow my dreams—even though they were not necessarily the dreams you and Dad had for me. I knew I always had your support!

You taught me, by your example, how to love and how to be loved. You taught me how to care for people and how to be worthy of having them care for me. You taught me how to be a Christian in life rather than in words only. You taught me that there is a positive for everything in life. Even in our sorrow, something good will ultimately come from the sorrow we are experiencing today.

I was always so proud of you! You were always such a lady. You also knew how to make us laugh and when we needed some alone time. You were always there for me. Even today, I feel your presence and know that you are watching over me.

I was so very fortunate to have you as my mother, my mentor, and my best friend! I love you so much and miss you terribly. I know you are in heaven and have made friends with everyone there.

Although there is still so much for me to do here on earth, I look forward to being reunited with you and Dad when God calls me home!

Thanks for listening. I'll talk to you tomorrow.

Love,

Lynette

5

# Sue Hammond

May 20, 2012

Plain Macaroni, No Cheese

A Letter to My Mother

I never blamed you, Mom. I always blamed Dad. But I've discovered through this assignment to write a letter to my mother that I have wildly convoluted feelings about you, Mom, not just affection.

I've gone deep into the onion of those feelings, peeling away layer after layer of love, hurt, sadness, grief, fear, disappointment, and insecurity, and in the rotten center was anger. I always felt sorry for you, Mom; I never realized I was also angry with you. Typically anger is a mask for other feelings. This time it happened in reverse. Oh, don't get me wrong, Mom, I do have anger, but it's never been toward you. It's always been elsewhere—myself, Dad, everybody else in and out of my life. At first I was worried about hurting you feelings by doing this project. I now see that I do blame you some, kinda . . . sorta . . . I think you had some responsibility for what happened to your children, despite your mental illness. You did have episodes of normalcy between episodes of insanity.

Yet you stayed with an alcoholic when you were given the chance to get us all back. Mom, he knocked you out and blacked your eye when you were nine months pregnant. But it was against your religion to divorce, so you chose Dad over us. Maybe you were insecure and knew you'd just keep losing it and we would continue to be taken away repeatedly anyway. That's what makes sense to me now. The other kids are not so forgiving.

You were full-blown bipolar type I with recurring psychotic episodes that required long stays in mental hospitals. Those doctors only saw you when you were psychotic. They didn't know what you had; they gave you shock treatments and antipsychotics. "I spent thirteen years of my life in mental hospitals. I added it up," you once told me, matter-of-fact, while chewing a sandwich with your mouth open and then coughing your brains out. I diagnosed you myself when you were sixty-five after watching a PBS documentary on the Amish and manic depression. The Amish always said, "It's in the blood," and they were right. They were the perfect group to study, a little pocket of people who married each other. The doctors listened to me. Once you were on lithium, you did better, but you still had to remain in a nursing home for sixteen years. You did time, too, Mom. I wonder if our lives would have been any different if your diagnosis had been made when you were young.

You left the Amish and Mennonite life when you jumped into a thirty-four-year marriage to a handsome alcoholic in uniform just back from the war when you were both twenty-three and proceeded to make nine babies. Dad would work all summer painting our small town in Ohio, stash two thousand dollars under the mattress, and proceed to drink it up all winter and make babies. "Your dad hated to work inside and have old ladies around bothering him," you said. Sometimes he would abandon the lot and run to "Mommy's in Kentucky" on a drunken binge or just disappear. That's why I blamed him all these years. Recently, however, I found out he wasn't a cook in the army; he was a medic. I have a little sympathy for him because he probably had PTSD. I don't know if stress got to you first and then he would leave or if he would start drinking and then you would fall apart. It probably happened both ways.

Did you ever consider how you were going to be able to raise all those babies? You weren't always out of your mind. I guess you lived in a dream world; you just loved babies. Your baby boy, number nine, miscarried, and you buried him in a shoe box under a cherry tree and begged God for another boy, saying, "I promise I'll raise him for Jesus!" Oh, you had another boy all right.

How did it happen that the older kids were in a children's home for five years 150 miles away and you were completely alone while you were pregnant with me and had infant Jackie and toddler Bobby with you living in some horrid shack? I know Dad was on a drunk and riding the rails out in Texas. A cop pulled him out of a bonfire that he rolled into because he was so drunk. Why were you alone all that time, starving?

Years later I'd say, "I found out I have a divided uterus, Mom. I might not be able to have kids."

You emotionally gushed, "Oh, I feel so terrible! It's my entire fault! I didn't have anything to eat but plain macaroni the entire pregnancy! I thought my milk wouldn't be any good for Jackie, so I only gave him (canned) evaporated milk his whole first year." Why didn't I think to ask you, "What did Bobby eat? Where were your five sisters? Were Dad's relatives living in the same area? Where was welfare? Come on! You must have been sick." To this day, Jack and I laugh and blame our health problems on the 'Macaroni Shack.' He's not laughing anymore; he's very sick. He's my favorite brother, the only one who ever cared about me.

You repeated that sorrowful confession anytime I mentioned some new health problem. So I stopped telling you because I didn't want to hurt your feelings. I believed your sad feelings and that you weren't playing the sympathy card. But what did I know? You were always the helpless victim. Things seemed to get back to your feelings a lot, Mom, not mine. I never realized that until this letter either.

Of course, the childhood trauma of repeated, sudden abandonment to strangers has fed a lifelong struggle with insecurity, feeling unwanted, and other issues for me. One day we would all be together and the next day we'd abruptly be taken away and separated to stay with a variety of strangers for six months to a year or two. This happened even when I was an infant. Then one magical day, just as suddenly, my childhood mantra, my wish that "we'd all be back together again" would be fulfilled. We never knew where we'd be from one day to the next.

This cycle repeated until we accidentally moved into a different county for three months when I was nine. That judge wouldn't put up with us. Bob, Jack, Annette, and I, the younger kids, became wards of the state of Ohio and the baby Jesus boy, Jimmy, was adopted. You swore you never signed adoption papers. Maybe you were sick and didn't know what you were signing. The judge even ordered one of you to be sterilized. Dad did it. "I felt so sorry for him. He was in terrible pain," you said. What about our pain? You refused to let Eve and Frank adopt me when I was five, whoever and wherever they are. It would have been a good life. You loved me too much.

The state of Ohio became my mother. She was one cold mother. We were sent to a state-operated children's home. There were 750 kids there. Annette and I were there until we graduated.

Jack and Bob kept running away and got out early. On graduation day we were told, "Five o'clock. Get off the grounds." There was no preparation for the outside world, no concern for where we would go. The state of Ohio was no longer my momma. One good thing came of it: I went to college. I don't think that would have happened if I had been raised at home, Mom, sorry.

Nobody noticed I had any abilities or intelligence until I was eleven and stuck in an abusive foster home and my teacher, Mrs. Betty Smith, took an interest in me and praised my artwork and grades. She put my poster of Egyptian women washing their clothes in the Nile where I had glued evergreen sprigs to the tops of palm trees into the lighted display case in the hallway, all by itself. Eureka! I thought, *"You mean I can get **praise** for getting good grades and doing art?"* That was it for me. I turned a negative into a positive thanks to that woman. After that, I aced almost everything, gained confidence, got a degree, and taught art for a while. I never got to tell you, Mom, that Mrs. Smith did that for me. Education was the way out. It was a way to feel like I mattered. To this day, I read and research constantly and own a huge library of books. Those books are more like family than my family.

Mom, I always felt you loved me, but it wasn't based on much. You sent me letters once a month when you were well when I was in the home and often a dollar. What a treat! My allowance from the state was sixty cents a month for what amounts to child labor. I'd buy a pack of gum, a barrette for my super long, straight hair, and maybe a candy bar. I had the longest hair in the home. Jealous girls cut off that hair one night in my sleep. I didn't cut it all short. I walked around with a couple of huge gashes of missing hair, which took three years to grow back out. Do you remember that?

And you wrote what a heartache it was for you that we were in that place. But Mom, you never visited once in all those years. We got out of that prison with no fence twice a year on vacation, but we didn't stay with you; we stayed with Marybeth, your oldest. That was not fun. You didn't come to my graduation because you had poison ivy. Few did. My siblings were just not that into me, like distant cousins only seen at funerals.

Hmm, let's see, what other evidence is there that you loved me? You told me secretly I was your favorite girl. "I never had to slap you once." You said I was the only one you were unconscious with during delivery. Nuns delivered me. The doctor was at a party. When you woke up, they told you, "Mrs. Hughes, you have a baby girl." You shouted out, "Oh, goodie!" You already had four boys but only two girls. Why did you keep wanting more? You just loved having children.

Oh, and when we were all together in the red brick house from my ages seven to nine, we'd come home from school and float through the door on a cloud filled with the smell of fresh-baked bread just from the oven. Our tongues would sweat as we buttered up our slice and slid that wonderfully warm gluten down our gullets into our happy bellies. We were together! We got Mom's homemade bread! Thanks, Mom, that was great. That was the Amish in you. You were a good cook and baker. But that's about all the mothering I remember. I don't remember hugs and kisses. Maybe there were some; I don't remember much about my childhood. I'm glad you told me stories about your life and mine.

Unfortunately, there's damage I have to let you know about, Mother, that I've read recently in new research studies. Turns out childhood trauma includes lack of nourishment in the womb. A diet of plain macaroni qualifies. Turns out, my organs were constructed with fewer cells, with made-in-China inferior parts from the dollar store. As a result, they have an early expiration date, a planned obsolescence attached to at least some of them. A baby being starved or malnourished while developing manages to make these cheap organs in order to survive and perpetuate the species. These children grow up fairly healthy but start having problems once they've accomplished their biological task of reproduction. By middle age they are wrought with a variety of mental and physical health problems, disorders, and diseases. The Dutch Winter Children, born during a WWII famine, now in their early sixties, are a prime example of this. Their life expectancy is not even decades close to one of a centenarian.

It also turns out that being tossed back and forth like a hot potato as an infant and child causes more than insecurity and low self-worth. It takes a heavy toll on mental and physical health too. PTSD is rampant among foster children, for example. Institutionalization doesn't improve the outcome. These children are sicker as adults than the general population, just like those starved babies in the womb.

Mommy, I've been sick since I was twenty-eight, right after the birth of my first baby boy. He was born two months premature. Remember that divided uterus? I had to stay in bed for five months to have my next son, two years later. I ate right. I didn't even drink coffee. I researched my tremendous responsibility. I loved those little babies like crazy and put all my effort into raising them well, despite spousal abuse. Today they are healthy, married, successful men living two thousand miles away. I got away from my abuser. I hope they stay healthy. They were small babies, and they saw some things. I haven't been a perfect mother, but I must have been good enough, they want their step-dad and me to retire out there.

I couldn't imagine giving them up. It was a love like no other in my life. But then, my bipolar disorder isn't as severe as yours. The anxiety disorder is another story. I had to stop teaching mostly due to chronic pain and fatigue. I'm middle aged now and have become much sicker in the past year. So far university specialists can't figure out what's up with the spots throughout my brain, double vision, small fiber neuropathy, loss of my sense of smell, and sudden short-term memory loss, with loss of my superb ability to spell any word I wanted. But I know the answer; chalk it up to cheap macaroni shack parts. I had to call my husband to learn how to spell *chalk* in the previous sentence. How does that stupid spell check work? I can't remember.

I'm sorry you spent sixteen years in a nursing home. We both did time, didn't we? I'm glad I visited regularly and got you out on weekends when you were well so the boys could know their grandma. They sure loved your cinnamon rolls and apple dumplings. They floated on that gluten cloud too. You sewed Raggedy Ann and Andy dolls that were sent to poor children all over the world by a church. I cherish the ones you made for my sons. For the last five years of your life, you could no longer walk. You quit sewing and stopped writing and collecting recipes in a notebook when your last one was lost after a breakdown. You just lay in bed watching television. That'll kill you, Mom. And so it did, fourteen years ago.

I couldn't tell you these things, the hard parts, while you were living. But despite the scattered thinking, confusion, and roller-coaster mood episodes, being bipolar isn't all bad. I am gifted with creativity and intelligence that has greatly enriched my life. I thank you for that. Once I designed fifty greeting cards in three weeks and made $8,000. But then depression came crashing in to spoil the party, and I never did it anymore. I'd be off on some new creative outlet when the bright lights came back on. I can't take psych drugs; I have several permanent side effects. I do better taking natural substances, but I still remain on the roller coaster, just not steepest one.

Without bipolar disorder, the world wouldn't have had the likes of Beethoven, Virginia Woolf, Vivian Leigh, Vincent Van Gogh,

Ernest Hemingway, Sir Isaac Newton, Edgar Allen Poe, Mark Twain, John Keats, Charles Dickens, F. Scott Fitzgerald, Mozart, Richard Dreyfuss, Patty Duke, Abbe Hoffman,. Dick Cavett, Jane Pauley, Mariette Hartley, Margot Kidder, Drew Barrymore, Charley Pride, Kurt Cobain, Amy Winehouse, Jessie Jackson Jr., Demi Lovato, and countless other writers, artists, and actors.[2] Even Winston Churchill's impassioned speeches that motivated a nation during a world war were given while he was manic. Genius and mental illness rub elbows.

And so, Mom, I thank you for my life. Without your love of having babies, I wouldn't be here. After all, I was number seven. I'm glad to be alive, for however long, on this pale blue spinning dot. Oh, and do you remember? My first word was *'cheese'*.

---

[2]  http://www.mhahc.com/PeopleIllness.htm;http://www.mental-health-today.com/bp/famous_people.htm and http://www.bipolar support.org/famous.html.

# Conversation with Sue . . .

## Why did you want to be part of the project and write the letter, and what did you get out of it?

I chose to participate in this project because of my love of writing and psychology. I'm interested in my mother and her choices. Writing has long been a passion of mine, along with photography and painting. I want to write a memoir, and this could get my feet wet. I knew the childhood sadness and loneliness would come through, but my matter-of-fact tone and sarcasm was interesting to discover. I learned a lot from doing this project. I highly recommend it.

I wanted to write this letter to my mother so I could examine her actions and choices intently to better understand her thinking. I also hoped to discover how her part in my life affected me. I never blamed Mom for only raising us for a few years on and off. Instead I felt sorry for her and her mental illness. After all, she wrote me heartachey letters with a dollar in them after we were taken away for good. I blamed Dad.

I came to realize that my mom chose Dad over us because she knew, at some level, that she couldn't raise nine children alone, welfare or not. The judge gave her the choice: him or us. She told us it was "against her religion to divorce," but she also knew she had had repeated mental hospitalizations since she was fifteen for nervous breakdowns. It's now clear that she was afraid to be alone. I can see how she might worry, even with a lack of knowledge about her condition. The first few bipolar breakdowns are triggered by heavy stress, but then the brain gets hardwired to just do it, sans Nike. In black and white on the page, I saw clearly that we would have continued to be torn apart as a family anyway.

I wish I had diagnosed her sooner than sixty-five. She did better once she was on lithium. Maybe our upbringing would have been less chaotic with at least one stable parent. Maybe she could have chosen her children and we would all be closer today. Life goes on.

I'm a bipolar mom too, but I limited my babies to two and focused completely on doing right by them. Now they live far away, and I miss them.

My mom's been dead for fourteen years now, and I didn't think to ask her, "What did Bobby eat? How did you end up alone in that macaroni shack with baby-bump me and two toddlers with no decent food to eat? Where the hell was everybody?"

I have many more questions.

6

## Your Second Daughter

Dear Mom,

If I could think of one word to best describe how you have been to our family, that would be *selfless*. I do not know of anyone else who is as selfless as you are. That quality has rubbed off on a few of us, but true selflessness is your badge of honor alone. Dad is a very blessed man to have you all these fifty-plus years to enjoy your kindness, love, humor, care, and great, great cooking, too! Not to mention bearing several children to rear and nurture. Those are not any easy jobs for anyone, but you do it with such grace and ease. I can remember over the years as we brought our friends home, many wanted to be part of our family, so they would adopt themselves to us. There was something there in our home that they wanted to attach themselves to. I realize that something was you.

Your strength of spirit, fairness, and determination are examples of the character that I had the pleasure of witnessing in you as I grew into womanhood. Even though I did not have children of my own, I do believe that I would have been okay with being a mom following your guidance and wisdom. It's funny because when I look at the different areas of our lives (i.e., food, clothes, books, music, home decor, etc.), we do not have very much in common. Nonetheless, the genes are very strong, and there is no mistake that

I am cut from a very fine cloth. I like the family we have become, and I hope and pray that the next generations hold onto the values that you and Dad instilled in us at a very young age.

While I watch as your body becomes a bit weaker and a little slower, it saddens me to think that you didn't get to do all of the things you may have wanted to do over the years. I'm not sure if you had a 'bucket list' but it would be cool to know what kind of adventurous ideas you had as a younger woman that may have been fulfilled or unfulfilled. However, your greatest joy is being able to have some quiet time with your book, a favorite TV show, or just taking a really long nap at home . . . uninterrupted.

Simple pleasures are always the best. That is my mantra too!

7

# Betty

## "Letter to My Mother . . . Why?"

I am writing this letter to my biological mom (Catherine Brown, a.k.a., Cat). I often wish I had another chance to talk to you and ask you all the unanswered questions, beginning with, "Why did you leave me at four days old? Why did you leave me, your first baby girl? I couldn't talk; did you even say good-bye? Did you ever worry about how I would be treated as a child?" When I had children, I worried about my children all of the time. When they grew up, I worried about whom they would befriend and the type of people they would become. I think back so many times and wonder why you would give birth to an innocent baby and then leave. Did you ever think that if you had the chance to get your little girl back, maybe you could be a good mother? A few years passed, and again I think if I had another chance to talk with my mom, I would ask her, "Did you ever really love me, even like me or wonder what I looked like? Who do I favor in your family?"

As I grew up, I thought so many times about how I didn't really know where I fit in or why I was staying with Theola McKinney (a.k.a., Theola), the only mother I would ever know. I was often around a lot of different people as a small child, and I would hear them say that you had given me to different people before. Why?

When I was a small girl in elementary school, the kids would say, "Do you know who your mother is?" Of course I did not. Did it ever occur to you that kids would be cruel to me and that I wouldn't have the answer to that question? I couldn't say yes. The only mother I knew and have ever known is Theola. She was my mom to me.

My mom, Theola, got married when I was six years old and left me with family members, Gilbert and Josephine McKinney. She moved to another home when she married Marshall Crawford. They lived on Red Line in Chesnee, South Carolina. One day I came home from school, and you were there waiting for me. You took me away. All Josephine told me as I was leaving was that I was going to live with my "real mom." I don't know or remember what I thought other than I had no choice in the matter. The one good thing that came out of it was that I found out that I had a little sister (Lula Mae, a.k.a., Cookie), and that made me happy.

The house you and your husband (Willie Mason) provided was a little place. He was a farmer working on someone else's property, and he drank way too much, so things were only stable for a little while. You came home from work one day with a white man, packed your clothes, and left us sitting on a bale of cotton that was on the front porch. Why? Why didn't you think of us? How were we supposed to survive? Did that ever concern you? We went to school looking very unkempt, and by the second day the teacher took us home with her because Cookie told her that she was hungry and hadn't seen her daddy.

As usual, things changed again. Cookie was taken to her grandmother to be raised, and I was taken to a cousin of my mom's. I had never met this person until I had to live with him. He was a child abuser who molested me every day! I was eventually returned to the person I considered my real mom—the person who had raised me from the time I was a baby until the age of six. If I could have asked you, Cat, my mother, just another question it would have been, "Why would you ever put your little daughter in such an unstable and abusive environment?" When I was returned to my original family, things got better because I was able to make new friends within my age group, and everyone who lived on Red Line was a mother figure. It was nice. I was a kid with lots of playmates. You know, Cat, as far back as I can remember, I wondered why so many things were different, but I was too young to know.

I suppose my father was an okay dad. Before I knew him as my dad, I just thought of him as someone who visited us and gave me money sometimes. Then I started to wonder about who he was, but no one told me, not even him. When I became a teenager, he continued to give me and my mom money all of the time. I can't tell you why, but one day I asked him why he always gave me money. He was very honest about it and answered as plainly as one could. He said that my mother (you) told him that he was my daddy. He said I looked just like his sister, so he guessed that I must be his. Finally, I look like someone in someone's family!

My mother, Theola, was a domestic worker during the day, and she ironed at night. She worked very hard all of the time. And although she never got to know how good I was in basketball in the eighth grade or see me play basketball, she always had my equipment ready. For that silent support from her, I was always so grateful. She didn't have the time to attend or support me in my school activities, but she made sure I knew that she was there for me, always. When school was out, I had chores. I learned how to care for all the animals my mom had. She was a very capable woman for her time. She had a farm with animals and a garden with wheat and corn, and she grew cotton too. I learned how to tend a farm every summer, right alongside of her.

A lot of years passed, and as a teenager I started to think of my future and wondered if I would get married someday. I hoped I would become a mom. I find myself wishing that I could talk to you and see what your advice would be to me. When I got married a few years later, I wished I knew what your thoughts would have been about your first son-in-law, but that wasn't possible.

As I write this story of my life, I start to wonder about a lot of things that happened in my life and whether you felt that me and my siblings were bad or ugly.

I am a grown woman now, and you are gone, along with all the other adults in this letter, so my "Whys" will never be answered.

If I could have a chance to talk to you, I would have at least a thousand questions as to what went wrong in your life. Why were you a runaway mom? But God has given me a forgiving heart, so I do forgive you. I wish I could ask you to explain all of the years that you missed out of your daughter's life, your grandchildren and your great-grandchildren's lives. And once you finished telling me and we stopped talking about the whys, then I would tell you the wonderful things you missed in all of our lives and how much love and devotion we all share.

# Conversation with Betty . . .

## Why did I want to be part of this project?

My son Jeffery was the one who wanted me to do this project; he wanted me to tell my story. I had a lot of people who did bad things to me when I was little and while I was growing up. My mother gave me away when I was four days old. I was also raped by a family member as a child. I don't want and have not let the bad times get the best of me. I know my life was unstable and at times abusive, but I think I turned out to have a good soul, and I'm quite funny.

## Why did you want to write the letter?

I'm seventy-four years old, and all of the people who did evil things to me have all passed away. My life has continued to prosper. My father was my mom Theola's first cousin, and I didn't find out who he was until I was between ten and a teenager. Then it all made sense to me why I was dropped off at her house as an infant. I have not led a rich life, but then I also have not led a poor life. My life has been good. I had children I loved and raised. I am a good-natured and loving person. I love my family and would do anything I could to help them if I could. The things I've written here I've not thought about for some time, and oddly enough, it still makes me wonder what was going on with my biological mother. I always knew things were not right, but I also didn't really know anything else. As for my real mom, Cat wasn't in my life enough for me to ever want to give her the title or call her mom.

## What did I get out of it?

The woman who raised and supported me (Theola) was the only person I ever considered to be my mom. After all is said and done, I give God all the credit because he watched over me during the struggles in my life. He is the one who placed the good angels in my life, and for that I can only feel blessed. It just makes me feel grateful to know that I was protected from above.

8

# D

Good morning,

It is at the request of a friend and with an anxious heart that I sit down to write a letter that is so far removed from anything I ever thought I would do. What would I say to you if given the chance? That was a question I never asked myself until recently, and now a million thoughts are going through my mind. I guess I should say that I feel thankful and blessed that, given the environment we were thrust into, all of us survived. We were somewhat bruised and battered for a while, but all of us had strong wills and giving hearts. That had to come from somewhere. On the surface, some of us may appear to be more scarred than others, but I am not sure that is the case. As I have grown closer to each of my siblings over the years, I realize that more and more. But we are all strong; we are not victims except of circumstance. We have lost two along the way, both sadly.

I think I remember the day you went through that door. What I remember the most about that day was my little brother at the door saying, "Please don't go." But go you did. He waited for you to come back, but come back you didn't. If I had been you in that day, in that time, maybe I wouldn't have come back either. My biggest question to you is this—knowing what you knew, why? Not why did you leave, but why did you leave us there? As I ask that question, I realize that you were but a child too. You needed to escape, and you couldn't take six babies. But you knew. Did it not matter? Did you not think about it? Did you hope and pray that it would be different? Of course on that day these were not my questions, but later . . .

I think you would have to have loved all of us—your children. You must have nurtured each of us and held us as babies, for I never felt that it was us you left. The thoughts and images that came to my mind when I would think of you and the time you were still there were not bad thoughts. I would remember a black-and-white floral dress with skinny straps and a warm and beautiful person wearing that dress. I remembered bits and pieces of songs being played over and over, and I still remember them to this day.

And then we were a close lot of siblings. We held onto each other. We loved each other with a fierceness sometimes that I know had to come about as a result of this life we were living. We could be mad at each other, but if someone else did or said something mean to any one of us, we stood together. This was especially true of our brother. From my earliest memories, I remember that we were always protective of each other. The three big kids and the three little kids. I don't feel badly about you. I always knew you were not coming home, but I often wondered why you never sent someone to make sure we weren't in harm's way.

The day that we were taken to the place that would be our home for the better part of our childhood was a blessing, although it was hard to know that then. For me, even though I never said this to the others at the time, I was happy to be going away—far away—as long as we could all stay together. I felt broken, and so as not to admit that to my siblings or even to myself, I buried some things so deep and decided I would never go there. I kept that promise to myself for a very long time. Some wounds, although hidden, never really go away. Jesus loves me, this I know. No one ever knew how much those little words to that song meant to me as a child. I don't think I really knew who Jesus was then, but I knew he loved me. As an adult and one who knows Jesus, I believe it was through his grace that this did not break me but truly made me stronger.

In closing, let me just say that forgiveness was the hardest emotion for me to grasp for so many years. How can you forgive what you don't understand? The heart that was shattered was finally healed when I figured out how to let go of those demons. I bear no grudges toward you. I am sure you fight your own demons. I know you went on to find someone to love and take care of you. And I am happy about that.

But I believe that somewhere deep in your heart, there must always be this bit of sorrow and regret for those you left behind. How could there not be?

With all due respect,

D.

Moral wounds have this peculiarity—they may be hidden, but they never close; always painful, always ready to bleed when touched, they remain fresh and open in the heart.

—Alexander Dumas

9

# Charmaine

Dear Mom,

Your memory of me is fading, and soon it will disappear. That saddens me greatly, although I never really knew you as well as I hoped to or thought I would.

I'm no longer in your womb, where your oxygen was my oxygen, where your food kept me alive. I have no memory of you feeding me at any point in my life, but you must have. I made it into the world. For that wonderful gift, I want to say "thank you, Mom, for life." My gift was turned over to the care of others, strangers, anyone up for the challenge. My small world was mostly made up of strangers. I was so little when you gave me away and gave up on me. I didn't even know for the first couple of years that you were absent. I didn't even remember you as my mother until you came to visit. When I did figure this out, I wanted to know, where do you live? How come I don't live with you? Don't you want me to? Don't you miss me? Do you love me? So many questions for such a little girl, yet they continued and haunted me through an important part of my life.

I often thought as I grew through all the stages of childhood, Why don't I have a real mommy? Why do other kids? Why doesn't my mommy want me? What did we do? I say "we" because I have lots of brothers and sisters, and we were scattered to the wind, as if one day a big gust of wind just swept us up and scattered us like leaves. As I grew up, my unstable life became even less stable and all the while I often thought about what you were doing. I did learn how to be responsible. At the age of ten, I went to go work in a steel factory to help my foster mom who was up in age, and although I never asked "Why?" it would have been nice if someone would have said, "She's just a little girl."

I wondered, were you ever going to come and rescue me? Didn't you miss me a little bit? I was sure you would like me a lot if you knew me. I needed a lot of rescuing when I was little, but I also learned that no one was going to come and I was on my own. No one explained to me how adolescence worked and what I should be prepared for, whether I wanted it or not. I was seldom, if ever hugged. I knew nothing about being hugged because someone loved me or was proud of me. There was no one to tell me I was loved. I didn't know if this thing really existed. What did I know about most things, Mom? There wasn't really anyone to teach me. What were you doing all those years? Weren't you supposed to teach me, help me?

You were like a shiny object, so pretty and bright, but you were just glances in my life. I had no way, no crystal ball, no magic words, and no time frame in which I would know when you would appear again. I wanted to spend time with you. I wanted to say, "Momma, can you see me?" but your visits were so overwhelmingly brief that it was as if you were a magician. My friends all seemed so lucky; they had moms who were wacky, sweet, serious, not so friendly, or just plain wonderful. To me, they all had what I wanted most—a mom—and I often fantasized about how that must have felt.

As a small girl, I would watch movies and disappear into the world of fantasy. You never knew that when I was a little kid I wanted Doris Day to be my mother. She had this big, bright smile, her singing was so pretty and she seemed so loving, just what I wanted my mother to be like. She was my pretend mother in my mind for a long time, and oddly enough, that gave me some happiness. They say the things that don't kill you will make you stronger. I don't know who *they* are, but I often thought I would die of a broken heart. My siblings were passing away, and I wondered if that was our fate—to be given away and then pass away.

God must have known I needed his help to soothe my disquieted soul even when I didn't know it. I was so determined to be something in my life because of the predictions of what lay ahead of me when I was little. I've worked really hard at it. I wanted to be everything that you were not, but you were smart, quick-witted, and knew how to survive, and so do I.

At different points in my life, I felt like someone was watching over me, protecting me, keeping me safe—preventing me from being too crazy or feeling resentment. I have a good heart and I borrowed my principles from people that I loved, looked up to, and encountered along the way. Surprisingly enough, I've got lots of love to give, and I've experienced wonderfully delicious relationships in my life and received so much love from them. This might not have all been possible if my life had been different.

Mom, I want you to know that sometimes I felt as if I was pushed past the point of breaking, but life has not made me bitter or hard. I embrace each day, value each relationship, and take nothing for granted. I feel fortunate to have had the experiences I've had and have learned from all of them. I'm forever the optimist but truly a realist. Although you weren't there to show me love, patience, and acceptance, others were, the best way they could. I didn't have any clear-cut example of the type of person I should strive to be, so I created myself like a tapestry, each weave hopefully better than the last.

When I graduated from college, I thought you would be so happy to be in the crowd celebrating my accomplishment, but you didn't come. When I was accepted into a graduate program at Georgetown, I knew that you had made up this "mother character" to your friends and co-workers' and liked to brag, so I was certain you would be in the crowd, but you weren't there. I was a grown woman and had been for years, yet the hurt and disappointment was so heavy and I knew better. I knew not to expect too much, but I remained hopeful in spite of my reality.

When I was a teenager and was in your rare company, I was the only one who used to ask so very many questions about *"why"*, *"how"*, and *"what happened to us?"* It used to set you off and you would hurl so many angry and abusive words at me that it felt like I was being hit with every angry thing that ever happened to you in your life. I never understood where the anger came from. I was just a kid trying to piece together my life. I had so many pieces of a puzzle that didn't fit anywhere, and I was just trying to figure out why. You'd come into our life and make all these promises and fade just as quickly. I learned how to look forward to your visit and not your words.

Now your memory is slipping away, like a thief in the night, and one day rolls into another. Each year is the same. We will never have that talk that I one day thought we would. I will never be able to hear most of your story. My mother, you will never be my best friend or my confidante. I have learned more during your illness than I ever did before. It's like all of your dark secrets are tumbling out, but you're no longer aware that they were secrets. I have desperately seized upon most of those moments, trying to hear your story, my story, our story. I am trying to understand the person you were, the choices you made. I was very touched when you grieved and felt despair about losing me when you thought I had passed away. In spite of your illness, you were going to miss me. I guess I knew then that you loved me, and maybe you always have in your own way. You have apologized for the pain you caused so many, me included. You have cried mournfully over things you have done. "I forgive you. It's all right . . . I'm fine."

I have long since forgiven you, Mom, and I have tried hard to be a very decent, honest, loving, and trustworthy person. A unique personality is how I'm described. I laugh easily, and I am a dreamer. If time had been on our side, you would have gotten to known all of these things about me. You once said to me when you first started realizing that you could not hold your thoughts, "You have shown me such kindness, more than I ever gave you. Thank you for helping me when I needed it. You are my little angel." Mom, regardless of your absence during most of my life, I have loved you from afar. I knew from a young age that I would help you and show you kindness that I may never receive. I've always been at peace with that because after all is said and done, without you, there would be no me, Mom.

Love,

Charmaine

You must be the change you wish to see in the world.
—Mahatma Gandhi

# Conversation with Charmaine . . .

### Why did I want to do this project?

The project originally was just me wanting to write down my thoughts to my mother that I was never going to be able to express because our relationship was always delicate and we never spent any substantial time in each other's company. I was very sensitive but tough when I was growing up.

It was hard for me to understand a lot of my mother's choices. I wanted her to want us—to be there, but she could never commit. When her senses became dulled, it was sad. I knew by visiting her and trying to get a handle on her medical condition that she would not remember most of what I was asking, but I did ask questions and took "lots of notes!" This letter allowed me to memorialize things I never had a chance to express.

### How did I choose these women?

When I thought of doing this project, I knew I didn't want to do it alone. I also knew that if I asked very special and close friends to do it, they had to be women of the same mindset in regard to wanting to expose a piece of their hearts. They had to be willing to pour their thoughts and emotions onto paper to be sampled and judged by a large audience of strangers to read and either be moved and enthralled by what they're reading or simply appalled. I initially was torn between women who played a big part in my life and who had some influence on who I became or women I had met in my travels and who I really enjoyed their friendship and company socially. I decided to send my invitation to a little bit of both! The one's I've shared so many highs and lows, tears and laughter, and confessions and goals with responded without hesitation. Well, there might have been one hesitant one. As mentioned earlier in the "introduction", these women who answered the call were all interested, excited, and nervous, but they are the writers in this book, and I do hope you enjoy their company and wisdom.

## What did I get out of it?

A lot! I know what real forgiveness is like and how hard it can be to unconditionally give it to someone who just never seemed to have enough time for you. It does not come overnight or easily, and for some not at all, but I was blessed to be able to forgive what I never had, wished I had, and missed. I accept things as they are now, and that is good enough.

I wanted to write this letter because I was removed from my mother's custody when I was four. My mother and I never really had a chance to have any heart-to-heart talks, although I tried many times. Now my mother has dementia, and although she still knows who I am and what my name is, everything else is jumbled up in her mind or has been tranquilly erased with the arrival of the illness. What she retained at the onset of the disease was a lot of memories from her childhood of her own mother and the love and approval she really needed from her. She did have a lot of memories of when my siblings and I were very small, almost babies, but instead of being absent, she raised us. My mom once described her inability to remember a sentence within minutes as "it washing away." I visit and check up on her regularly. She has no clue whether I'm coming or going, but I have to have a clear conscience after all is said and done.

She still knows my name, but she doesn't associate it to me entirely. I hesitate; well, I am not brave enough at this time to find out what my relationship to her is or who she thinks I am. A couple of years ago she referred to me more than once as "a very nice lady," and she thinks we could be good friends, a relative of one my sisters, or the one who saved her from her loneliness. She commonly refers to me now as *little Charmaine*. We are friends, even if we are no longer mother and daughter. I don't know what her eyes see, and I get lost in her memory, so I enter her world during my visits and leave mine behind for a time.

My opportunities to have a heart-to-heart have long since passed now, so I put my thoughts down on paper so I can express our relationship, my hurt, my sadness, my forgiveness, and ultimately my survival. Like everyone else, my experiences color my world and make me who I am.

My mom liked for the camera to be pointed in her direction, so I'm sure she'd be amused and flattered that she was the reason for this book. My mother was not an integral part of my life, but I always wanted her to know more about me, be proud of me. I hope that somewhere in her mind, she is.

# Poems

Submitted by Vickie, one of the Writers
(This is a poem my daughter Jennifer
wrote me her senior year of high school.)

She doesn't like to cook, but it isn't all that bad; I have my mother's legs—and for that I'm very glad

She's a protective mom; she says I'll thank her someday, but I can't understand why I can't have my way.

She's there to cheer me on at every single game. It makes me proud when people say they think we look the same.

I wouldn't be the same without her as my mother; she even picked my dad and had my sister and brothers.

She loves her cappuccino and lots of books to read. Somehow she always knows when people are in need.

She inspired me to run and taught me to eat right. When young she taught me manners and how to be polite.

She gave me her advice—if I wanted it or not. She never let me win in all the times we've fought.

She loves to decorate; our house is never done. I think it looks like work, but I think she thinks it's fun.

She took me to my church and taught me how to pray. She showed me how to live my life in a Christian way.

I think my mom is great and that she deserves more credit. I hope she knows I love her, even though I've rarely said it.

## My Mother

She's probably a lot like any mother.
She perfected the art of worrying.
She is an expert at ESP.
She passed the gift of gab to the next generation.
She's my mother!

She is independent in her thinking.
She always stands up for her beliefs.
She is a tower of strength yet as gentle as a lamb.
She's my mother!

She doesn't always understand why I do the things I do.
She doesn't always like the things I do or the way I do them.
But—
She always accepts me.
She's my mother!

She taught me to look at all sides of people and situations.
She taught me to be patient with people and situations.
She taught me the gift of unconditional love.
She's my mother!

She has supported me when I failed.
She has praised me when I succeeded.
She has shredded my hopes and dreams.
She's my mother!

She has been my nurse and chauffeur.
She has been my teacher and mentor.
She has been my friend.
And best of all—
She will always be *my mother*!

Written by Lynette A. McMillen, 1995

# Afterword

The purpose of the book was to allow friends who are so close to me that they are my family to express things to their mothers that maybe they never had the chance to, wished that they had said more, were willing to say, or needed to say now! As a result of these open letters and raw expressions put to paper, a lot of tears were shed and eye-opening revelations were experienced. When you write with your heart and soul, it can be very painful, very healing, or both. Some women were initially afraid that they would hurt their deceased mothers' feelings; some never had any interest in communicating any further with their mothers at all, while others wanted to get some things off their chests! As a result of wanting to compile these letters, I have a better understanding of my friends then I ever thought, and I always thought I understood all of them pretty well!

When I assembled these letters, I felt their pure, unadulterated love for their mothers and the pride and respect some felt toward someone who had influenced them so greatly and helped shape them. Some of these letters clearly state "how these women became who they are" and how they wanted to be an asset to society and those around them. I was caught off guard by the nagging and intense loss and how much some of them still longed for their mothers' comforting words and influence. This degree of love, I must say, was foreign to me, yet it was wonderful to know that it existed and some of my friends had lived it and experienced it. I was truly touched by all of the women's humbleness and ability to remember things that made you laugh or brought you to tears. I was awed by their forgiveness towards their mothers who were not part of their life or never came back. The questions and attempts to understand why their lives was derailed at such an early age or not at all were so telling.

This book is not to imply that fathers are not important—they are—but it was written to recognize and identify the people, the source, and the individuals who brought us into the world. The purpose was to acknowledge these women, regardless of whether they loved us beyond our wildest imaginations and when we think back and about them, our memories are flooded with the same kind of happiness a kid feels on Christmas, or whether, for whatever reason they gave up on us at a time when we were too little or so vulnerable that it was hard to comfortably adapt to our surroundings and fully grasp the totality of our loss. However, intuitively, we knew something was wrong and missing because our worlds did not resemble what we largely saw around us.

Every writer expressed that these letters—letters that you read—ultimately provided them with some inner peace, and if this book provides you with the same peace or encourages you to memorialize the words in your heart or your head, then we have indeed "paid it forward".

# What's the Story on Some of the Writers?

### *Charmaine Sheeler*

Charmaine Sheeler is a native of Ohio and is one of ten children. When she was a little girl she was always trying to "create something" and had the imagination to go along with it. Being one of ten kids you can get lost in the shuffle but she always remained positive. Since collaborating with her friends to write this book, her mother's health has deteriorated and she is grateful that she was able to express their relationship. She believes that every child should start out with the warmth of family but knows that is not always the case. Her goal is to allow people to read about women that are self-sustaining, productive, resourceful individuals in society, whether they came from a normal family, or not.

### *Chimére L. Smith*

Growing up, Chimére L. Smith always heard elementary school teachers rave that she was one of "brightest students in the classroom, but she sure does talk a lot." And while many things have changed, those observations certainly have not. But Chimére also now ranks finishing what she starts high on her long list of priorities. In 2010, after four years of being prodded by family and friends, she begin to pursue her dream of becoming a makeup artist and has provided beauty and grooming services to Grammy-nominated clients and worked alongside Emmy-winning makeup artist Reggie Wells of *The Oprah Winfrey Show.*

She was also recently named beauty editor of the growing blog *The Diary of a Natural Gal,* a web-based publication that highlights the strengths of African American women in education, fashion, beauty, and entertainment. She's also completing her education at Morgan State University in Baltimore, Maryland, with a BA in English. If you ever want to find Chimére, she'll either be buried under a good book, rustling through clearance clothing racks, or applying makeup to some of Washington, DC's, most prominent women. And you can guarantee that she'll be talking the entire time.

### Caren J. Pringle-Gray

I was born and raised in Canton, Ohio and currently lives in Oakwood Village, Ohio, with my husband Robert of nine years. Our family consists of three young-adult children (ages sixteen to twenty-two), our three-year-old grandson, and a five-year-old boxer. I received my BA and a graduate certification in HR management. Currently I am employed at the world-renowned Cleveland Clinic as an absence management office representative. I own a successful wedding/event planning business (established 2004).

My mother, Minnie L. Pringle-White, died in July of 1986 from a very long and painful battle with lung cancer. The oncology doctors told us she had six months, but she fought to survive nearly two years. I believe she hung on to make sure that all five of her children were settled. Secretly, once she was diagnosed, she purchased all sort of items for all of us, in particular furniture. She did this so we would be able to start building our own homes. Now, twenty-six years later, I would like to think my mother is proud of me, what I have accomplished, my family, and the home life I have tried hard to model after what she has taught me. She gave me a solid foundation, and for that I'm forever grateful. I am honored to have been her daughter, and I am humbled by the experience of having her in my life.

### Sue Hammond

Sue lives in Springfield, Ohio, with her husband, Dwight, and four cats, three of which were dumped on their country property. Her backyard is a nature preserve. She has two sons, Zach and Grant, who reside in Las Vegas. She taught art in public schools until she had kids. She's taken a number of creative writing courses, and her professor said, "Publish!" She hopes to take creative writing workshops or get an MFA one day. She loves writing, photography, and painting and has sold paintings and photographs, but this is her first time in print. Writing has taken over as her primary passion, even more so as her mobility decreases. She recently took a trip out west for her son Grant's wedding and is planning to go up Highway 1. She needs and seeks the beauty and fresh photography opportunities. She wants her body of work to be appreciated, not thrown out with the trash. Maybe there's still time. She needed a mother.

### Lynette A. McMillen

Lynette is married, and she and her husband, Larry McMillen, live in Folsom, Louisiana. They have four children and five grandsons. She is the eldest of four children from Bettie and Sam Allgood. She was born and raised is Louisiana, and with the exception of one year in Houston, Texas, and two years in Washington, DC, she has lived in Louisiana her entire life.

Lynette enjoys scuba diving, writing poetry, needlework, walking, biking, and playing Sudoku. Her greatest joy comes from being around family. Her mother passed away in 2005 from a rare lung disease, just two months prior to Hurricane Katrina. Her father passed away in 2010 from complications of a brain tumor, which caused a massive stroke, just twelve days before his eighty-fourth birthday. Her siblings and their families, along with Lynette and her family, try to get together annually or at least biannually so the nieces, nephews, great-nieces, and great-nephews will remain connected—hopefully throughout the rest of their lives.

Lynette has a special interest in helping the youth of St. Tammany Parish and the surrounding areas. She has volunteered at Children's Hospital, Covenant House. She was a substitute teacher for a third-grade class. This is where Lynette learned a little bit of sign language. She has taught her five-year-old grandson a few words and letters in sign language. She would like to become proficient in the language and feels everyone should know basic words and phrases in this magnificent language. One of her other rewards while a substitute teacher was substituting for the remedial English class at the local high school. Asking the students to rewrite the poems and plays in verbiage they used every day not only allowed her to know that they understood the "wherefore" and "thou," but it also allowed them to have a voice and to appreciate the language and culture of the time

Lynette was a schedule C appointee in President George W. Bush's administration. It is Lynette's hope that you will be able to see a glimpse of the wonderful life and relationship she had with her family, especially her mother, as you read her letter and poem. She says, "I wish everyone could be as blessed as I have been by having parents, siblings, a husband, a child, stepchildren, grandchildren, and friends who have always been and continue to be my inspirations. My Lord, Jesus Christ, has given me more love than I deserve. I hope that through the love and inspiration from everyone, I may help make a positive difference in someone else's life before I leave this earth. Thank you for the opportunity to share a glimpse of the mother I love and miss with all of my heart."

### The Anonymous Writers

The other writers are made up of professional women who work in the fields of nursing or administration. They live very active lives filled with lots of love from their husbands, children, grandchildren, friends, and family. Some of these women also operate small businesses, and as you can see from these moving letters, they all are intelligent and have a voice.

# Bibliography

*105 Writing Tips from Professional Writers.* 2006.

http://timesoak.com/post/17378339388/105-writing-tips-from-professional-writers.

Angelou, Maya. *Letter to My Daughter.* New York, NY: Random House, 2008.

Bipolar Disorder Today. Available at http://www.mental-health-today.com/bp/famous_people.htm

Goldberg, Natalie. *Writing Down the Bones: Freeing the Writer Within.* Boston, MA: Shambhala, 1986, 2006.

James Patterson. The Official Web Site. September 2006/2012.

http://www.jamespatterson.com.

Kebani, Shama Hyder. *The Zen of Social Media Marketing.* Dallas, TX: BenBella Books, Inc., 2010 2012.

Mental Health America of Hendricks County. http://local.yahoo.com/info-15887215-mental-health-america-of-hendricks-county-avon /December 28, 2012. http://www.mhahc.com/PeopleIllness .htm.

Poynter, Dan. *Self-Publishing Manual, Vol. 2.* Santa Barbara, CA: Para Publisher, 2009.

—., Bingham, Minday, Conrad, Barnaby. *Is There a Book Inside of You? Writing Alone or with a Collaborator.* Santa Barbara, CA: Para Publisher, 2007.

Stevenson, Jay, Ph.D. *Pocket Idiot's Guide to Grammar and Punctuation.* New York, NY: Penguin Books, Ltd., 2005.

Rich, Jason, R. *Self-Publishing for Dummies.* Hoboken, NJ: Wiley Publishing, Inc., 2006.

http://www.bipolarsupport.org. 2006/2011. http://www.bipolarsupport .org/famous.html

Self-Publishing and Other Resources

Dan Poynter's ParaPublishing.com. 2006/2012. http://www. parapublishing.com/

Tate Publishing; Publishing Your Book, Publishing Companies. 2004/ 2012. http://www.tatepublishing.com

Made in the USA
Lexington, KY
02 November 2017